3

Cornell's carefully constructed cabinet with compartments, corks and a cockatoo

Inspiration
on his doorstep

A photograph of South Broadway, one of the main streets in Nyack, taken around 1900. Life in this quiet town was very different from that in New York City

The Cornell family home where Joseph spent much of his happy childhood, photographed around 1915

Joseph Cornell was born in 1903 in Nyack, a little town about 30 miles north of New York City along the Hudson River's western shore. He lived there all his life. He used to read a lot, and in his imagination visited many far-off lands. Much of his art is based on a love of Europe and of traveling, even though he barely ever left New York.

He frequently journeyed into New York City in search of inspiration. He knew it very well and loved every aspect of it, from the shop windows to the cafés, from the museums to the second-hand stalls where he could find old movie magazines and postcards.

4

During Cornell's lifetime, building was going on at breakneck speed in Manhattan, the heart of the city—moving ever upward. In 1902, the year before he was born, the highest structure was the Flatiron Building, with twenty stories. Just twenty-nine years later, the Empire State Building was completed, with 102 stories (1472 feet high).

Backwards and forwards by train between Nyack and New York City, Cornell was always on the lookout for interesting things to collect

Higher and higher: the Fuller Building, 41 East 57th Street at Madison Avenue, New York, 1929

Reaching for the sky: Madison Square, New York, 1929

The constantly changing skyline could be seen from the train, and as he walked around the streets. Whenever he was in Manhattan he explored the galleries and libraries and went to exhibitions, often picking up souvenirs which he used later in his work. He particularly loved the city at dusk, when the neon lights from shop windows and cafés spilled out into the street.

Coins, stamps, shapes, and circles: this collage is known as *Penny Arcade with Horse*

5

What did Cornell make?

All Cornell's works are made up of interesting bits and pieces put together in an unusual way. What is more, all the materials he used are ordinary, everyday things.

His first works were collages, made by sticking lots of different images onto a board. He often decorated the back of the collage too—this means that in order to see the whole work properly, it has to be turned over.

Cornell started making boxes to display things in the late 1930s. At first glance it might seen as if he made them quite casually; in fact they were very carefully constructed. He worked on certain ideas again and again—using similar materials—just slightly changing the way in which the objects were laid out. There is one series of boxes showing different birds, and others based on themes such as the hotel or the planets and stars. Sometimes his ideas overlap and the same images can be found in different series. He was particularly fond of birds, shells, and clay pipes.

Toward the end of his life Cornell made a number of detailed collages, often dedicated to filmstars. The images are a mixture of photocopies of famous works of art and magazine pictures, photographs of film stars, and pages from books.

6

The Tiara, one of the artist's late collages, picks up again on the themes of planets and circles

This box of mysteries with lots of different compartments comes complete with a collage on the door

How to spot a work of art by **Joseph Cornell**

- His boxes are sometimes like pieces of furniture with doors and drawers.

- He had a number of images that he loved to use: shells, eggs, pictures of film stars, images of the night sky or maps of the stars, parrots and owls, pictures of women in late 19th-century dress—or any combination of these.

- Other artists made collages, too, but Cornell seldom cut up the images he used. So if there is a text from a book or magazine you can probably read it, and the pictures cut out to be part of the collage (e.g. of birds and people) were used whole rather than in part.

- When other artists use such a variety of different materials, their works often seem threatening or violent. When looking at a Cornell work there is a feeling of dreamy calmness.

- Cornell loved structure: his boxes are very carefully fitted out, and his collages precisely cut so that images are joined together rather than overlapping.

What was Joseph Cornell interested in?

Every one of Cornell's works is packed with fascinating details. Most of the things he included in his work he had collected on visits to New York City. He spent many hours looking through second-hand shops for old advertisements and keepsakes and had a big library of books and magazines. Everything he collected he catalogued and stored carefully until it was needed.

Because he kept referring to the same subjects in his work, it is interesting to look at these in a bit more detail.

Ballet

Cornell loved the ballet and often went to watch. He saw the famous prima ballerina Anna Pavlova dance and collected information on several other stars.

Butterfly wings, beads and glitter for a ballet star

8

Mixing words and pictures as in theater, opera, or cinema

Opera

Joseph and his sisters often went to the opera, sometimes buying "standing room only" tickets at the Grand Metropolitan Opera in New York. He put together several folders with articles and pictures on famous opera stars both of the time and of years gone by.

Theater

The stage was something else that particularly impressed Cornell. His parents had been keen on amateur theatricals and he enjoyed all sorts of shows from "Punch and Judy" to formal productions. The influence of the stage set can be seen in many of his works.

9

Cinema

The fascination of the cinema: (left) the artist looking at a poster showing Greta Garbo, and (above) his work of art with photos of Lauren Bacall

Cornell loved to go to the cinema and watched both silent and talking films. He collected film material and also wrote and produced some short films of his own.

This "constellation", generally known as the *Solar Set*, was made around 1956–58

Astronomy

As a frequent visitor to the Hayden Planetarium at the American Museum of Natural History, Cornell subscribed to its magazine Sky Reporter. He had over thirty books in his library on astronomy, and used the word "constellation" to describe his method of working.

In 1951, he wrote about what he thought when looking at the sky : "The expansiveness of the heavens, the song of nature, the breezes, the fragrances of the grasses—like a great breathing—deep, harmonious, elemental, cosmic."

Books

Cornell had a huge library of books, guides and maps. Sometimes he cut up pamphlets and magazines to create his images, but he always made sure that you could still read the words.

This book cover was designed by Cornell himself in 1936, based on an advertisement he had drawn a few years earlier for an exhibition of the same name

Exhibitions

The artist was a frequent visitor to the many exhibitions and galleries in New York City, and loved to collect old exhibition catalogues and publicity information.

Dutch paintings and the Old Masters

Cornell's family was originally from Holland and he was very drawn to the 17th-century Dutch paintings by the famous artist Vermeer. These paintings often show a scene inside someone's house, with all sorts of interesting items brought together in one space. Vermeer was also very skilled at painting light.

Johannes Vermeer, *The Glass of Wine*, 1658–60: such perfectly painted pictures with their mass of detail were an inspiration to Cornell

A beautiful portrait in a new setting: Cornell's box construction,
generally known as the *Medici Slot Machine*

19th-century illustrations

Images of 19th-century women wearing elegant dresses made a strong impression on Cornell, and such pictures often find their way into his work. Dresses were held in shape by frames and layers of undergarments.

Floating high above the mountain peaks: Cornell's work *Tilly Losch,* made around 1935

The Church

In 1925 he joined the Christian Science Church and remained an active member for the rest of his life. He was influenced by the writings of the Christian Scientist Mary Baker Eddy, who emphasized how important it is to be open to inspiration.

Toys

Old toys, in particular Victorian toys which were part puzzle and part entertainment, had always fascinated the artist. He loved things that would appeal to his disabled brother Robert, such as train sets and puzzles.

Based on a fairy tale called the *Snow Maiden*, this box whisks us away into the magical world of the winged child

Stars, a bull, a pipe and blue sand: a mysterious dream-like mixture of images which could have all sorts of different meanings

Surrealism

This was an artistic movement which was popular when Cornell first started showing his work. He admired the Surrealist artists, and was influenced to a certain extent by them. Surrealist artists combined all sorts of different images in their paintings aimed at producing a reaction in the viewer, these images often being found in our dreams or in our minds.

Birds

Colorful cockatoos and parrots occur in many of his works, as well as solitary owls. Cornell found the details of their migratory journeys very inspiring as this linked with his own fascination for astronomy and navigation.

Grand Owl Habitat,
made around 1946

There was something about hotels that captured Cornell's imagination. The contrast between the busy lobbies and the isolation of all the independent travelers in their lonely rooms upstairs was something he found intriguing.

Look carefully at the notice behind the parrot and you will see that this is also one of the artist's "Hotel" boxes, *The Hotel Eden*, from around 1945

Think Box

Every artist takes the things he or she finds intriguing as a starting point. Imagine you are an artist and make a list of all the things you find really fascinating. What you choose is up to you, but try to be really specific. You could take a particular style of advertisement you have seen, activities you enjoy after school or programs you enjoy watching. Here are some of the author's favorites to get you started:

- Furniture from the 1930s, in particular things made of walnut—a golden colored wood
- The 1960s television series 'Bewitched'
- The color yellow

Looking at a Cornell work more closely

Having seen where the images in Cornell's work come from, let's take it a stage further and look at how they relate to each other. This box has a variety of different things in it, all of which have some sort of connection with one another although this may not be so obvious at first glance.

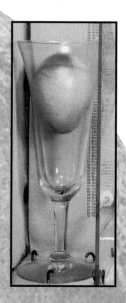

Take a closer look at all the round things. There is a map of the moon, the head of a child, the top of the glass and its base, the ends of the cylinders at the top, and the round pieces of glass at the bottom of the box.

How do these things work together? The bubble pipe is placed so that you could imagine that the moon has just come out of it. The egg is a "stretched" circle, of the kind that comes out of a bubble pipe just before floating off into the air. Even two of the cylinders at the top have circular images on them, the low flying planet and the halo around the horse's head.

This box, popularly known as the *Soap Bubble Set*, combines many of Cornell's favorite themes: a map of the moon, a clay pipe, circular objects and the mystery of the universe

CARTE GÉOGRAPHIQUE DE LA LUNE

Any number of things have been used to make up this collage.
This is a close-up of part of *Encrusted Clown* (see page 2)

Why is Cornell's art the shape it is?

Even when first put on display, Cornell's work was unusual. Today, too, it is certainly not what most people would expect to see in an art gallery or on the walls of their home.

Collage is an old art form, but was also favored by the Surrealist painters in the 1930s, such as Salvador Dalí. Joseph Cornell also wanted to make people think more closely about how we see things in the world around us, and record images we see in our dreams.

Why did Cornell like using boxes?

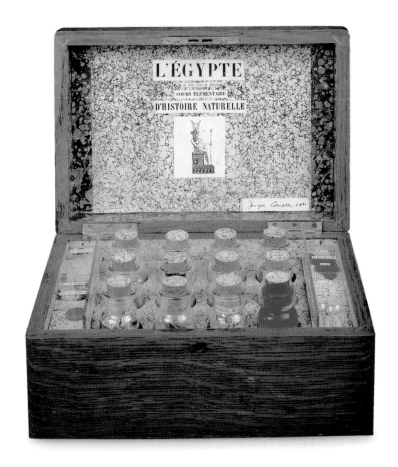

A lot of people have tried to find an answer to this question. As we have already seen, he was very attracted by the theater and we can see the influence of the stage in many of his compositions. Sometimes Cornell positions the objects against a backdrop rather like a stage set behind the actors in a theater production.

Cornell's structures could be either cabinets or deep boxes like this one. He invites us to take out the bottles and have a closer look. The bottles contain a strange mixture of objects such as a doll's arm, a wooden ball, little pieces of a broken mirror, stones, shells, sand and many other interesting things.

Think Box

What did Cornell like?

- Furniture with doors and drawers that hide some things and reveal others
- Dutch painting where everyday items can be seen in detail
- Puppet theaters
- Old French puzzle boxes
- Glass-sided clocks, and watches with glass backs, so that you can see the moving parts
- Toys that are in boxes—in which they can be played with or simply kept in when not in use

Expecting the unexpected

Untitled (Bébé Marie), made
in the early 1940s

There is a real sense of mystery and magic in much of Cornell's work.

Sometimes you wonder what has just happened; what is the story behind the image we see?

For example, in the box on the left, why is the doll behind the twigs?

Is she trapped in an enchanted forest?

If so, why does she look so calm?

When did this happen; how long has she been stuck there for?

Question upon question ... but there are no answers!

Cornell made many boxes in which birds are sitting on perches but in this one there is no bird. The wire mesh netting has been opened (rather than forced). Has something just escaped, and if so, what was it and where has it gone? And who opened the netting? The box is just a fragment of a story...

22

Toward the "Blue Peninsula," 1951–52

Untitled (Pink Palace), 1946–48

Sometimes the sense of mystery lies in the way Cornell combines items that don't really belong together; things seem to float around in a dreamy landscape. Other works have a sense of mystery; the maps of groups of stars—or constellations, as they are called—give a huge sense of scale, yet on the other hand they are combined with tiny everyday objects such as buttons or bits of shiny paper. Treating everyday objects as great treasures gives them a very special magic.

Upside-down and back-to-front: this is the back of the box shown at the bottom of page 15. If you look closely you will see that Cornell signed this work in mirror writing

How to look at Cornell's work

Cornell wanted his work to make people curious. This is art that is meant to interact with the viewer, not just to be looked at. For example, the extracts from real magazines and newspapers are always readable, and this draws the viewer in for a closer examination.

This door belongs to the box on page 7 and shows a collage of pages of text and images taken from the romantic French story *Paul and Virginia*

He encouraged people to touch many of his works, to get involved in thinking about what is behind the mysterious doors and in the compartments. The collages too work best if you really get close to them and examine what materials he has used.

The ship's compartment box on the right has a lid that covers all the individual sections. The lid can be removed to reveal what is inside, or left in place so the contents can only be glimpsed at. It's like a sailor's bag, full of mysteries from long journeys at sea.

The backs of many of his works are also decorated, so the object has to be turned around in order to be seen properly. Others can be moved around and the contents taken out in order to be appreciated. What is more, when the items are moved, the sound made is also meant to be seen as part of the work.

Mapping an adventure: Cornell covered this collection of objects with a lid. Normally we can only peep through the holes into the little compartments but here the lid has been taken off to show the contents inside

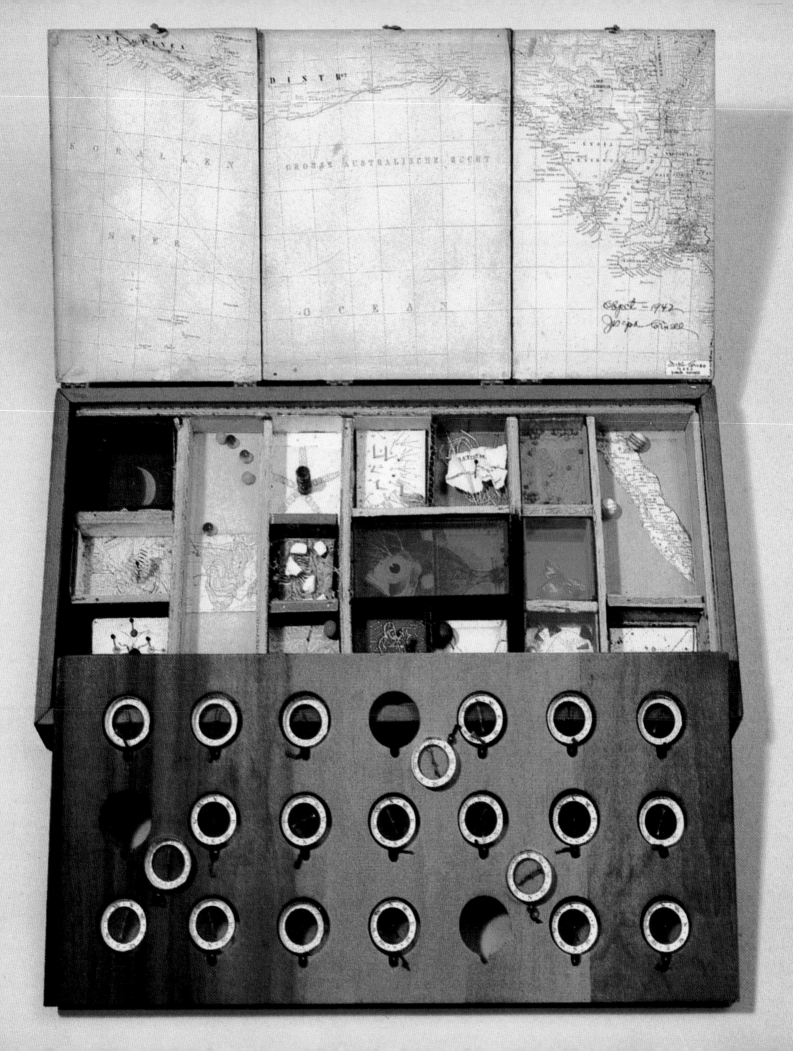

More about the artist's life

Joseph Cornell was the eldest of four children. He had two sisters, Elizabeth and Helen, and a brother Robert, the youngest. The family was well-off and his parents were musical and enjoyed taking part in local concerts and plays. He had a very happy childhood. His grandparents lived next door, and birthdays and Christmas were celebrated with special family traditions, such as hanging up paper decorations made by his mother.

Cornell's father died in 1917 and this was the start of a very difficult period for the family. They had to leave their big home and move house many times over the next few years. Joseph stayed on at school until he was seventeen and then left to get a job to support his family. He was not particularly successful at school and there are no reports to say that he was especially interested in art. He got a job in the textile industry, but he was shy with the customers and did not enjoy the work. However, when traveling to New York to sell the company's wares, he began to wander around the city.

It is not known exactly when Cornell started making works of art, but one day when visiting a gallery, he showed the owner his collages. The gallery owner liked them and included some of Cornell's work in his next exhibition. In 1940 he decided to become a full-time artist.

He lived with his mother and brother for most of his life, working from his studio in the cellar of the family home, where he not only produced his work but also kept the materials with which he worked, all carefully catalogued according to subject matter or type of object.

26

Joseph Cornell died at home on December 29, 1972. He was sixty-nine years old.

27

Make your own Cornell Box in six easy stages!

1 Think about what to put in your box

Look back to your list of favorite things on page 17, and try to collect as many bits and
pieces as possible. You could make a box:
• to remind you of a fun day out (at the circus,
  a hike in the country, or a shopping trip)
• to show what you did on your last vacation
• about your hobbies
• about a filmstar or a pop group

2 Start collecting

Look for objects that you find interesting. Collect more
things than you need and then spread them out on a table.

3 Sort out the best objects to use

Return to your collection a few days later and think what you
want to include. Which pictures and items link together and
will be interesting to someone else looking at your box?

4 Choose your box

A shoe box or a chocolate box works well, or you could make your own. Perhaps you will want to cover your b
first—do you want this to be part of the finished item? Decorate your box (outside and inside or just inside). You
could staple or stick items to the back of the box or you could make a shelf or two out of cardboard or twigs.

5 Fix your collection in the box

Place your pictures and items in the box and see how they relate to each other. Look and see how carefully Cornell's
items have been positioned. Think about what you want the person looking at your box to do—should they move it
around or just examine it closely. If you want items to move you will have to think carefully about how to affix ther
Fix everything in place once you are happy with your work of art.

6 Give your finished box a title

And what date will you put on it, if any? The day on which you finished it or the day on which you had
the best idea for what it should look like? Now you can sign it—and your Cornell box is complete!